Presentation by *BookLeaf Publishing*

Web: www.bookleafpub.com

E-mail: info@bookleafpub.com

ISBN: 978-93-5744-357-9

First edition 2022

DEDICATION

Dedicated to my father, who taught me how to write and has encouraged me every step of the way.

the beginning, part one

Lessons are learned like slips of paper collected
in a jar for safekeeping
They could be torn, crumpled, crisply folded
covered in dirt or the shards of heartbreak it took
to collect them

But they are all paper

All cut from an experience as large as a tree,
delicately condensed into
an object to keep in your palm until the ink
absorbs
into your skin
or stuck into your back pocket to be forgotten
about
or put in the jar

The ones in the jar stick
Those are the lessons we remember

the beginning, part two

I didn't always have a jar
First, it was an undecipherable mess of paper
scattered throughout my room
easily misplaced
and easily

forgotten
To be out of mind doesn't have to be out of sight

Paradoxically, it took a lesson to learn lessons
I learned to keep track of the pieces of paper I
gathered
and I found a jar to keep them in

Because a jar can't forget

The less important lessons I keep in my bag
protected, yet accessible to help me remember
But the jar keeps the important ones

I have a total of six in the jar. They are as
follows:
    acceptance
    truth
    invisibility

names
consent
& beauty
We will begin with acceptance, because isn't that
the beginning of everything?

acceptance, part one

Definitions:
1. to receive
2. to be received

Contranym- a word
depending on the context
means its opposite

Difficult concept
for a young girl to master
thanks to influence

Such as society's
message: Survival of those
who learn to conform

And rejection of
those who don't want reshaping
to be what they're not

All the girls seem copied and pasted
Individuality is wasted

acceptance, part two

I wasn't bullied
Only ignored by many
But I prefer that

Because I've realized
The best people are the ones
that don't care like me

Deeper belonging
is what we crave, our little
posy of misfits

"There are friends, there is
family, and there are friends that
become your family."

I'd rather be loved for someone I am
Instead of "allowed" for something I'm not

acceptance, part three

So I sit and watch
as all the comparison,
so called "acceptance,"

Tears people apart
Breaking down all that was so
carefully built up

Desperately trying
to find anything that could
possibly save them

Acceptance is a
difficult lesson to learn,
don't you remember?

When everything is said and done
No one is a prize to be won

truth, part one

At first, I was the most naive
Full of dreams and young
Everyone I would believe
Ignorant to their fun

But my blind trust proved a fault
Became my Achilles heel
I learned to tell the true from false
The stories from the real

To trust is good when given to
a person honest and safe
But then I got lost in my misconstrue
Nothing's real with one who's fake

"Time can heal," is what they say
"Time discovers truth."
But instead of finding reasons to stay
I found lies inside of you

truth, part two

Lies are lies, big or small
And all the while I knew
People talk a lot to stall
So I watch what they do

In a twisted way, there's something sweet
And something real to find
About listening to lies on repeat
When I know the truth behind

I wouldn't take back what you've done to me
Being used and abused and mocked
I learned to trust imperfectly
The door's only closed, not locked

My vision's clear, my heart is sound
From any more betrayal
I add the lesson, folded and bound
To my jar upon the table

invisibility, part one

"Be seen and not heard."
repetitive the words
we're told as we play
amongst the fray
and to this day
we're older and wiser
but all of these guys are
treating us like kids
in boxes with lids
waiting to be sorted
stamped and exported
to the next reported
place with a job
to be done by a mob
but some of us know
when to put on a show
and when to be gone
invisibility drawn
silent like a pawn
voices withdrawn
survival mode on

invisibility, part two

We've learned to hide
to stay inside
the walls around
and hide our sound
but then we've found
sometimes it's better
to ignore the fetter
and speak our minds
without the binds
ring out our words
like mockingbirds
unto the herds
catch the attention
give something to mention
and make a change
rules rearrange
because being heard
over lines that are blurred
is sometimes a need
that needs to be freed

names, part one

"What's in a name?" So the saying goes
But I don't believe that names mean nothing
There's a power behind your reputation
That when used wisely, could leave your mark
On the world, whether good or bad

Under your name, you make friends or foes
Either by telling the truth or bluffing
The most effective method's dictation
For news or advertising, it ignites a spark
So recheck your numbers for the launchpad

names, part two

I follow the rules of the wolf pack
The keys are determination and respect
Those who fall behind are condemned
But I take a slightly more merciful view
Turning opposition into opportunity

1. If they stand in front of you, watch their back
2. If they stand beside you, give them respect
3. If they stand behind you, protect them
4. If they stand against you, break through
But why choose to defeat when there's power in
unity?

names, part three

13

A single kind action or conversation
I've learned is mighter than sword or pen
When trying to change anything
And make something of yourself
In a world so easily affected

Cruelty and apathy plague our nations
Breaking us down over and over again
So I want to be the one to face everything
Stare it down in the eyes myself
Because we will no longer be subjected

consent, part one

In this world of old and young
I've noticed differences between girl and boy
When it comes down to words off tongue
Men sometimes think it's all a ploy

When you try to hold my hand
Why don't you understand
If I go to pull it away
Clearly that is not okay

consent, part two

15

"No" doesn't mean to try again
or try harder with different strategy
"No" simply means "no," my friend
I won't change my mind with flattery

Look, you're sweet and a really grand guy
But this is where I say goodbye
I won't stand to be ignored
Because you need to have a reward

consent, part three

I admire your courage, sir
But I'm afraid it's been misplaced
I'm not as easy as the other girls were
And I'm also not double-faced

I'll be honest with you for sure
But please don't be immature
When I say, "Don't do that please,"
That is not me trying to tease

consent, part four

So if we ever reencounter
Please remember these words I say
Don't sit there again and flounder
Trying to find another way

I haven't forgotten how you treated me
The way you though I was for free
Existing entirely for you to play
A game with, well, sorry, not today

beauty, part one

Joy doesn't have to come from big grand things
The birth of a first-born daughter or son
Or a marraige proposal with gold rings
Followed by a wedding: "You shall be one."

No, I've learned from a world with little joy
That to find happiness, you must look close
Turn everything into a small child's toy
By looking through lenses tinted with rose

I choose to find the beauty and pleasure
Power of perspective is my treasure

beauty, part two

Pretty lights at Christmastime, tiny birds
Standing out in the rain, the smell of pine
Pink clouds, dancing, snowball fights, spoken
words
These are the many pleasures I call mine

Not all moments are sunshine and roses
Some days seem just a little bit colder
But happier will be the one that knows:
"Beauty lies in the eye of beholders."

So I'll stay looking on the sunny side
Happy with my tail bushy and eyes wide

to write

The art
Of putting

Words to paper that
Readers fall
In love with and
Take into their
Existance

to read

The art
Of

Receiving what is written and
Engaging in stories
And
Dreams

to dream

The art
Of

Daring to
Realize the impossible and
Enjoy the
Adventures we
Make for ourselves